© International Music Publications Ltd
First published in 1999 by International Music Publications Ltd
International Music Publications Ltd is a Faber Music company
Brownlow Yard, 12 Roger Street, London WC1N 2JU
Music transcribed by Barnes Music Engraving Ltd
Printed in England by Caligraving Ltd
All rights reserved

ISBN10: 0-571-52577-6    EAN13: 978-0-571-52577-5

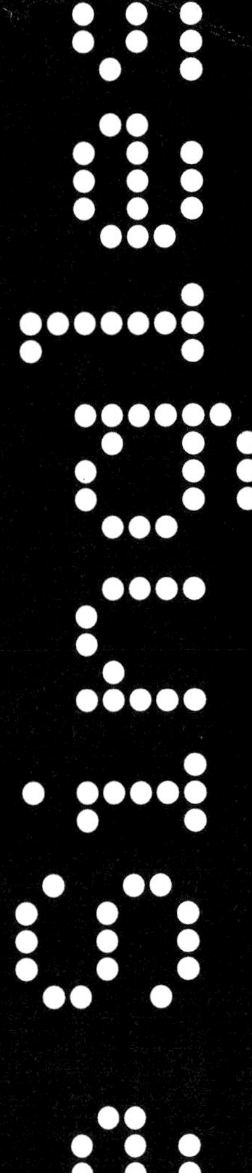


6    Stripped

11    A Question of Lust

15    A Question of Time

23    Strangelove

28    Never Let Me Down Again

34    Behind The Wheel

40    Personal Jesus

45    Enjoy The Silence

49    Policy of Truth

56    World In My Eyes

60    I Feel You

65   Walking In My Shoes

72   Condemnation

74   In Your Room

79   Barrel of a Gun

85   It's No Good

91   Home

96   Useless

101   Only When I Lose Myself

108   Little 15

114   Everything Counts


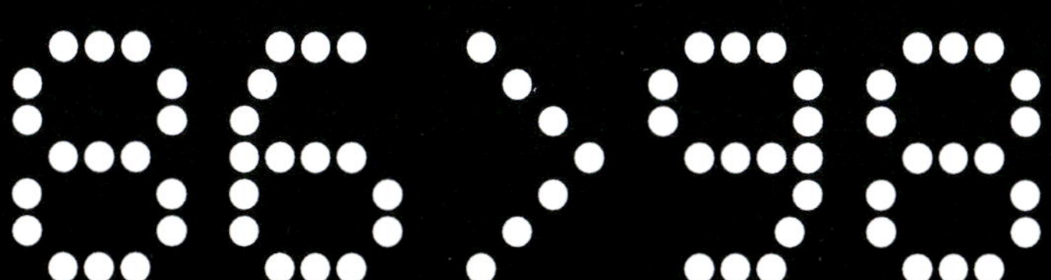

# Discography 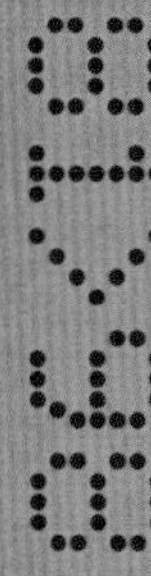

### Dreaming of Me
Released: 20th Feb. 1981 / UK chart position: 57 [Mute 13]

### New Life
Released: 13th Jun. 1981 / UK chart position: 11 [Mute 14]

### Just Can't Get Enough
Released: 7th Sep. 1981 / UK chart position: 8 [Mute 16]

### See You
Released: 29th Jan. 1982 / UK chart position: 6 [Mute 18]

### The Meaning Of Love
Released: 26th Apr. 1982 / UK chart position: 12 [Mute 22]

### Leave In Silence
Released: 16th Aug. 1982 / UK chart position: 18 [Bong 1]

### Get The Balance Right
Released: 31st Jan. 1983 / UK chart position: 13 [Bong 2]

### Everything Counts
Released: 11th Jul. 1983 / UK chart position: 6 [Bong 3]

### Love In Itself
Released: 19th Sep. 1983 / UK chart position: 21 [Bong 4]

### People Are People
Released: 12th Mar. 1984 / UK chart position: 4 [Bong 5]

### Master & Servant
Released: 20th Aug. 1984 / UK chart position: 9 [Bong 6]

### Blasphemous Rumours/ Somebody
Released: 29th Oct. 1984 / UK chart position: 16 [Bong 7]

### Shake The Disease
Released: 29th Apr. 1985 / UK chart position: 18 [Bong 8]

### It's Called A Heart
Released: 16th Sep. 1985 / UK chart position: 18 [Bong 9]

### Stripped
Released: 10th Feb. 1986 / UK chart position: 15 [Bong 10]

### A Question Of Lust
Released: 14th Feb. 1986 / UK chart position: 28 [Bong 11]

### A Question Of Time
Released: 11th Aug. 1986 / UK chart position: 17 [Bong 12]

### Strangelove
Released: 11th Aug. 1986 / UK chart position: 17 [Bong 13]

### Never Let Me Down Again
Released: 24th Aug. 1987 / UK chart position: 22 [Bong 14]

### Behind The Wheel
Released: 28th Dec. 1987 / UK chart position: 21 [Bong 15]

### Everything Counts [Live]
Released: 13th Feb. 1989 / UK chart position: 22 [Bong 16]

### Little 15
Released: 16th May. 1988 / UK chart position: 60 [Little 15]

### Personal Jesus
Released: 29th Aug. 1989 / UK chart position: 13 [Bong 17]

### Enjoy The Silence
Released: 5th Feb. 1990 / UK chart position: 6 [Bong 18]

### Policy Of Truth
Released: 7th May. 1990 / UK chart position: 16 [Bong 19]

### World In My Eyes
Released: 17th Sep. 1990 / UK chart position: 17 [Bong 20]

### I Feel You
Released: 15th Feb. 1990 / UK chart position: 8 [Bong 21]

### Walking In My Shoes
Released: 26th Apr. 1993 / UK chart position: 14 [Bong 22]

### Condemnation
Released: 13th Sep. 1993 / UK chart position: 9 [Bong 23]

### In Your Room
Released: 10th Jan. 1994 / UK chart position: 8 [Bong 24]

### Barrel Of A Gun
Released: 3rd Feb. 1997 / UK chart position: 4 [Bong 25]

### It's No Good
Released: 31st Mar. 1997 / UK chart position: 5 [Bong 26]

### Home
Released: 16th Jun. 1997 / UK chart position: 23 [Bong 27]

### Useless
Released: 20th Oct. 1997 / UK chart position: 28 [Bong 28]

### Only When I Lose Myself
Released: 7th Sep. [Bong 29]

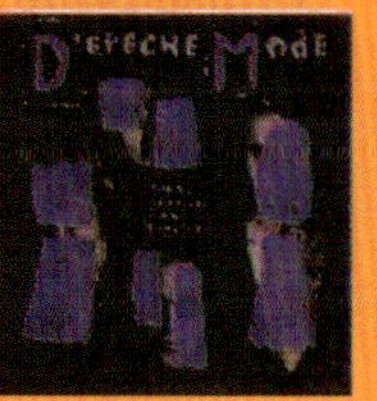
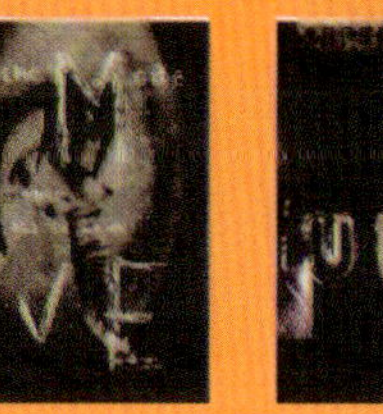

## Speak & Spell
Released: 5th Oct. 1991 / UK chart position: 10 [MCDSTUMM 5]

New Life
I Sometimes Wish I Was Dead
Puppets
Boys Say Go!
Nodisco
What's Your Name
Photographic
Tora! Tora! Tora!
Big Muff
Any Second Now [voices]
Just Can't Get Enough

## A Broken Frame
Released: 27th Sep. 1982 / UK chart position: 8 [CDSTUMM 9]

Leave In Silence
My Secret Garden
Monument
Nothing To Fear
See You
Satellite
The Meaning Of Love
A Photograph Of You
Shouldn't Have Done That
The Sun & The Rainfall

## Construction Time Again
Released: 22nd Aug. 1983 / UK chart position: 6 [STUMM 13]

Love, In Itself
More Than A Party
Pipeline
Everything Counts
Two Minute Warning
Shame
The Landscape Is Changing
Told You So
And Then...
Everything Counts

## Some Great Reward
Released: 24th Sep. 1984 / UK chart position: 5 [STUMM 19]

Something To Do
Lie To Me
People Are People
It Doesn't Matter
Stories Of Old
Somebody
Master And Servant
If You Want
Blasphemous Rumours

## The Singles 81>85
Released: 15th Oct. 1985 / UK chart position: 6 [MUTEL 1]

Dreaming Of Me
New Life
Just Can't Get Enough
See You
The Meaning Of Love
Leave In Silence
Get The Balance Right
Everything Counts
Love In Itself
People Are People
Master And Servant
Blasphemous Rumours
Somebody
Shake The Disease
It's Called A Heart

## Black Celebration
Released: 17th Mar. 1986 / UK chart position: 3 [STUMM 26]

Black Celebration
Fly On The Windscreen - Final
A Question Of Lust
Sometimes
It Doesn't Matter Two
A Question Of Time
Stripped
Here Is The House
World Full Of Nothing
Dressed In Black
New Dress

## Music For The Masses
Released: 28th Sep. 1987 / UK chart position: 10 [STUMM 47]

Never Let Me Down Again
The Things You Said
Starange love
Sacred
Little 15
Behind The Wheel
I Want You Now
To Have And To Hold
Nothing
Pimpf

## 101
Released: 13th March. 1989 / UK chart position: 7 [STUMM 101]

Pimpf
Behind The Wheel
Strangelove
Sacred
Something To Do
Blasphemous Rumours
Stripped
Somebody
The Things You Said
Black Celebration
Shake The Disease
Nothing
Pleasure Little Treasure
People Are People
A Question Of Time
Never Let Me Down Again
A Question Of Lust
Master And Servant
Just Can't Get Enough
Everything Counts

## Violator
Released: 19th Mar. 1990 / UK chart position: 2 [STUMM 64]

World In My Eyes
Sweetest Perfection
Personal Jesus
Halo
Waiting For The Night
Enjoy The Silence
Policy Of Truth
Blue Dress
Clean

## Songs Of Faith And Devotion
Released: 22nd Mar. 1993 / UK chart position: 1 [STUMM 106]

I Feel You
Walking In My Shoes
Condemnation
Mercy In You
Judas
In Your Room
Get Right With Me
Rush
One Caress
Higher Love

## Songs Of Faith And Devotion [Live]
Released: 6th Dec. 1993 / UK chart position: 46 [LSTUMM 106]

I Feel You
Walking In My Shoes
Condemnation
Mercy In You
Judas
In Your Room
Get Right With Me
Rush
One Caress
Higher Love

## Ultra
Released: 14th Apr. 1997 / UK chart position: 1 [STUMM 148]

Barrel Of A Gun
The Love Thieves
Home
It's No Good
Uselink
Useless
Sister Of Night
Jazz Thieves
Freestate
The Bottom Line
Insight

## The Singles 86>96
Released: 28th Sep. 1998 [MUTEL 5]

Stripped
A Question Of Lust
A Question Of Time
Strangelove
Never Let Me Down Again
Behind The Wheel
Personal Jesus
Enjoy The Silence
Policy Of Truth
World In My Eyes
I Feel You
Walking In My Shoes
Condemnation
In Your Room
Barrel Of A Gun
It's No Good
Home
Useless
Only When I Lose Myself
Little 15
Everything Counts [Live]

# Stripped

Words and Music by
Martin Gore

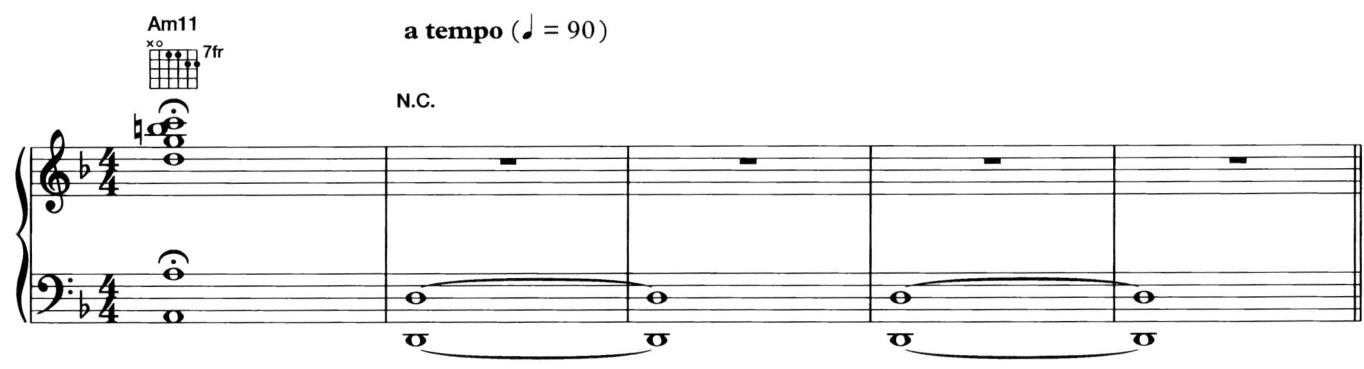

A5    Dm    A5    Dm/C
let's go a-way___    just for one day.___    Let me    see you    stripped
Dm/G    Dm/B♭    Dm
___    down    to the    bone.___
Dm/C    Dm/G    Dm/B♭
Let    me    see you    stripped___    down    to the    bone.___
Dm

Dm
A5
Me-tro-po - lis___ has no-thing on this,___ you're breath-ing in fumes___ I
Dm
A5
Dm
taste when we kiss.___ Take my hand,___ come back to the land___ where
A5
Dm
A5
Dm/C
ev-ery-thing's ours___ for a few hours.___ Let me see you stripped
Dm/G
Dm/B♭
Dm
___ down to the bone.___

Dm/C
Dm/G
Dm/Bb
Let me see you stripped_ down to the bone.___
Dm
Dm/C
Dm/G
Let me hear you make___ de - ci - sions___
Dm/Bb
Dm
Dm/C
_ with - out your te - le - vi - sion.___ Let me hear you speak-
Dm/G
Dm/Bb
Dm
- ing just for me.___

Dm/C    Dm/G    Dm/B♭    Dm
Let me see you stripped down to the bone.__ Let me hear you speak - ing just for me.__
Dm/C    Dm/G    Dm/B♭    Dm
Let me see you stripped down to the bone.__ Let me hear you cry - ing just for me.__
Dm/C    Dm/G    Dm/B♭    Dm
Let me see you stripped down to the bone.__ Let me hear you speak - ing just for me.
Dm
1st time only
repeat to fade

# A Question Of Lust

Words and Music by
Martin Gore

Emaj7
C#m
F#m
E
me. ____________________ But just like a child, ________
one. ____________________ It fright-ens me. But I need to drink more than

F#m
E
G#m
you make me smile when you care for me, and you know ... It's a ques-tion of lust,
you seem to think be-fore I'm a - ny-one's, and you know ...

A
B
G#m
__ it's a ques-tion of trust. __ It's a ques-tion of not __ let - ting what we've built

C#m
B
A
G
C
Am
B5
to Coda
__ up crum - ble to dust. __ It is all of these things __ and more that keep us to - ge - ther.

1.
2.
Em6
2. In-de-
Kiss
A
Emaj7
A
B
N.C.
D.%. al Coda
me good-bye_ when I'm on my own, but you know that I'd ra-ther be home._ It's a ques-tion of lust,
CODA
A
B
G#m
4fr
It's a ques-tion of lust,___ it's a ques-tion of trust.___ It's a ques-tion of not___ let-ting what we've built
C#m
4fr
B
A
G
C
Am
B5
_ up crum-ble to dust.___ It is all of these things___ and more that keep us to-ge-ther.

It's a ques-tion of lust,
it's a ques-tion of trust. It's a ques-tion of not let-ting what we've built up crum-ble to dust.
It is all of these things and more that keep us to-ge-ther. It's a ques-tion of lust,
repeat to fade

# A Question Of Time

Words and Music by
Martin Gore

Ab
Eb
I've got to get to you first, ___ it's just a ques-tion of time.
Gm
1st time only
F
1.
2.
Gm
F
Well now you're on-ly fif-teen ___ and you look good. ___
Gm
F
I'll take you un-der my wing, ___ some - bo-dy should.

Cm
They've per-sua-sive ways___
and you'll be-lieve what they say._
Ab
Eb
Cm
__ It's just a ques-tion of time____
Ab
Fm
and it's run-ning out_ for you.____
It won't be long un-til_
Gm
Ab
Bb
N.C.
_ you'll do_ ex-act-ly what they want you to.____

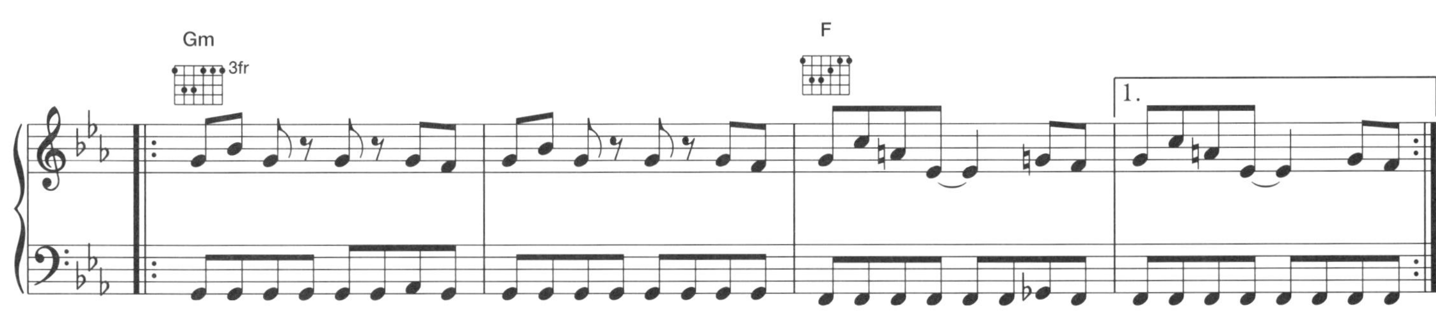

Gm
F
1.


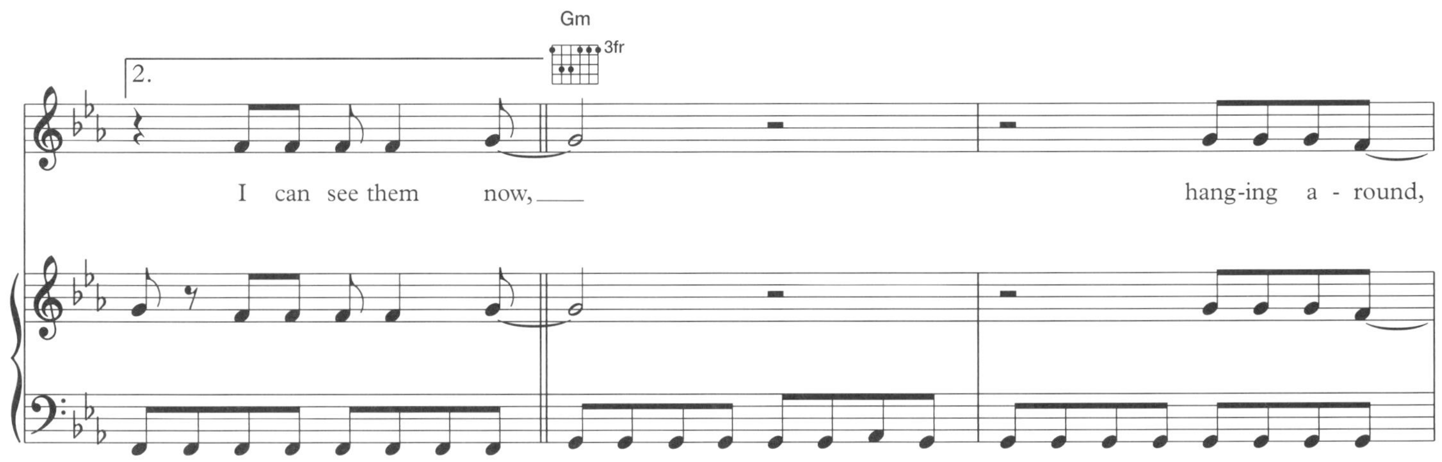

Gm
2.
I can see them now, ___          hang-ing a - round,

F
Gm
___          to mess you up, ___          to strip

F
Cm
___ you down          and have their fun ___

with my lit-tle one. It's just a ques-tion of
time and it's run-ning out for you.
It won't be long un-til you'll do ex-act-
-ly what they want you to. It won't be long un-til
Ab
Eb
Cm
Ab
Fm
Gm
Ab
Bb
Fm

Gm
Ab
Bb
N.C.
__ you'll do ex - act - ly what they want you to. ____
Gm
F
1.
2.
Some-times I don't blame ___ them for want-ing you. ___
Gm
F
Gm
F
You look good ___ and they need some-thing to do. __

Cm
Until I look at you
and then I con-demn them.
Ab
Cm
I know my kind,
Ab
Eb
what goes on in our minds.
It's just a ques-tion of
Gm
F
time,

Gm
F
it's just a ques-tion of time.
Gm
It's just a ques-tion of time,
it should be
F
bet - ter.
It's just a ques-tion of time,
Gm
F
repeat to fade
it should be
bet - ter with you.
It's just a ques-tion of time.

# Strangelove

N.C.
Em
and will you re - turn it?
omit 2nd time
C
Am
Em
C
Am
1. There'll be times
2. There'll be days_
Em
C
when my crimes_ will seem_ al - most un - for -
when I'll stray.__ I may ap - pear to be__ con - stant - ly

Am
Em
-giv - a - ble. I give in______ to sin______ be-cause you
___ out of reach. I give in______ to sin______ be-cause I
C
Am
Em
have to make this life live - a - ble. But when you think I've had e-nough from your
like to prac - tise what______ I preach. I'm not try - ing to say I'll have it
C
Am
sea of___ love,_ I'll take______ more than an - o - ther ri - ver - ful. Yes and
all my___ way, I'm al - ways will - ing to learn when you've got some-thing to teach. Oh and
Em
D
Am
Bm
C
D
I'll______ make it all______ worth - while, I'll make your heart smile.
I'll______ make it all______ worth - while, I'll make your heart smile.

N.C.
Pain will you re-turn it, I'll say it a-gain, pain.
1.
2.
Em
Pain will you re-turn it, I'll say it a-gain,
C    Am    Em
pain. Pain will you return it,
C    Am
I won't say it a-gain.

Em
Am
Am/C
Em
Strange - love, strange highs and strange lows. _ Strange - love,
Am
Am/C
Em
Am
Am/C
that's how my love goes. _ Strange - love, will you give it to me. _
Em
Am
Am/C
Em7
Strange - love, strange highs and strange lows. Strange - love,
repeat to fade
Am
Am/C
Em7
Am
Am/C
that's how my love goes. _ Strange - love, will you give it to me.

# Never Let Me Down Again

Words and Music by
Martin Gore

D5
C5
G5
I____ hope he ne - ver lets me down a-gain.
D5
C5
G5
B♭maj7
He knows where he's tak - ing me,__ tak-ing me__ where I____ want to be.__
D5
C5
G5
I'm tak-ing a ride____ with my best friend.
D5
C5
G5

Cm
Bb
Gm
We're fly-ing high,___ we're watch-ing the world___ pass us by.___
F
Cm
Bb
___ Ne-ver want to come down,___ ne-ver want to put my
Gm
F
D5
feet back down on the ground. __
C5
F
Eb

31
D5 C5 G5
I'm tak-ing a ride___ with my best friend.
D5 C5 G5
I___ hope he ne - ver lets me down a-gain.
D5 C5 G5
Pro - mi - ses me___ I'm as safe as hous - es, as long as I re-mem-ber who's
B♭maj7 D5 C5
wear-ing the trou - sers. I hope he ne - ver lets me down a-gain.

G5
D5
C5
G5
Cm
Bb
We're fly-ing high, __ we're watch-ing the world
Gm
F
Cm
pass us by. ___ Ne - ver want to come down,
Bb
Gm
F
1.
F
__ ne - ver want to put my feet back down on the ground. __

33
2.
F
Dm
C5
A5
Gm
Dm
C5
A5
Gm
Dm
C5
A5
Gm
Ne-ver let me down,___ ne-ver let me down.___
Dm
C5
A5
Gm
repeat to fade
See the stars, they're shin - ing bright, ev - ery-thing's al - right___ to - night.

# Behind The Wheel

Words and Music by
Martin Gore

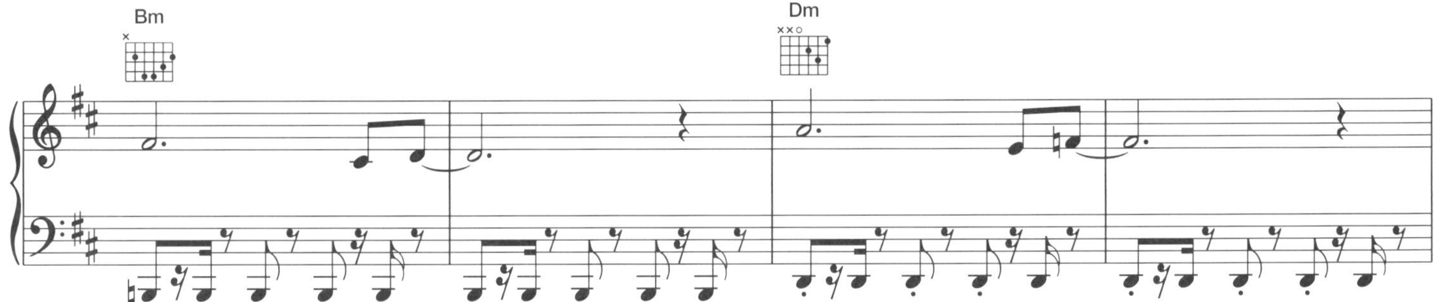


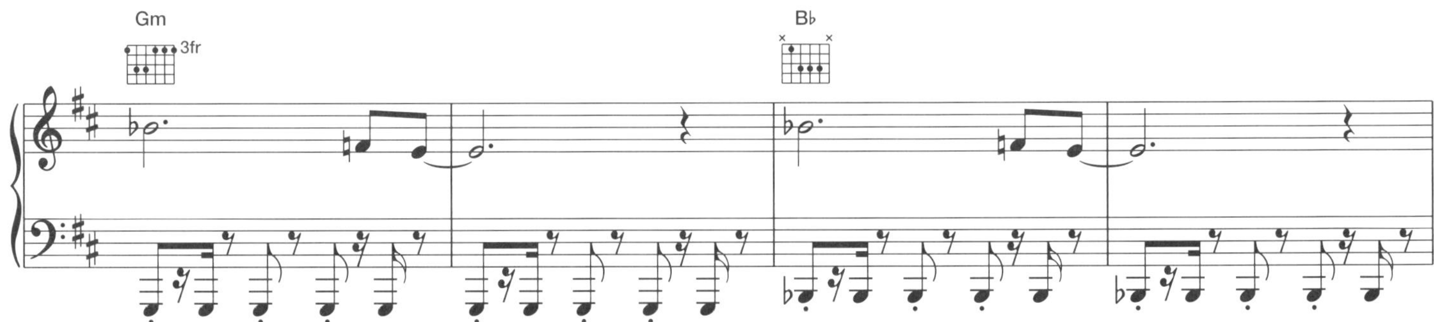


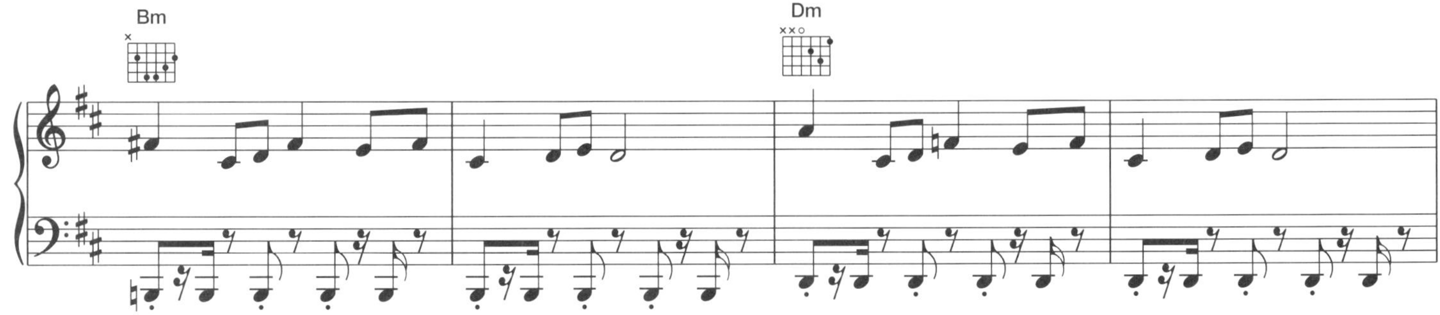

Gm
Bb
1. My lit-tle girl,
Bm
Dm
drive a - ny - where,
(2.) there are times when I feel
(3.) I pre - fer
Gm
do what you want,
I'd ra - ther not be
you be - hind the wheel
I
the one
and me
Bb
Bm
don't care.
be - hind the wheel.
the pas - sen - ger.
To - night,
Come,
Drive,

Dm
I'm in the hands of fate,___
pull my strings,___
I'm yours to keep,___
I hand my - self___
watch me move,
Do what you want,
Gm
Bb
o - ver on___ a plate,
I do a - ny - thing,
I'm go - ing cheap,
to Coda
Bm
now.
please.
to - night.
Dm
Gm

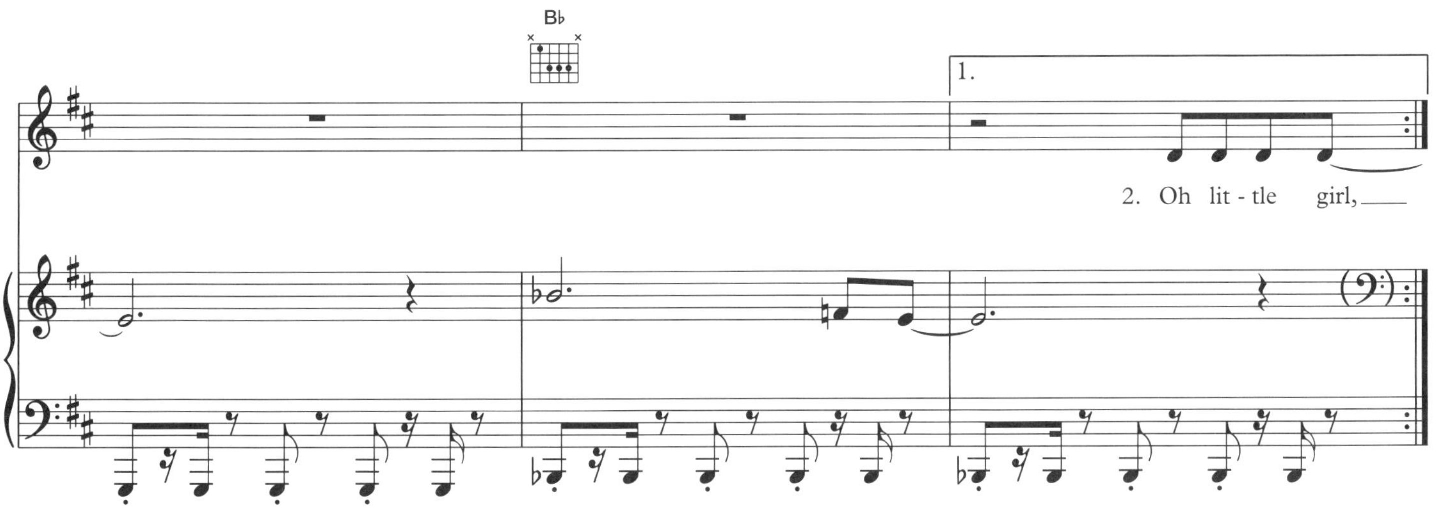
Bb
1.
2. Oh lit - tle girl,____

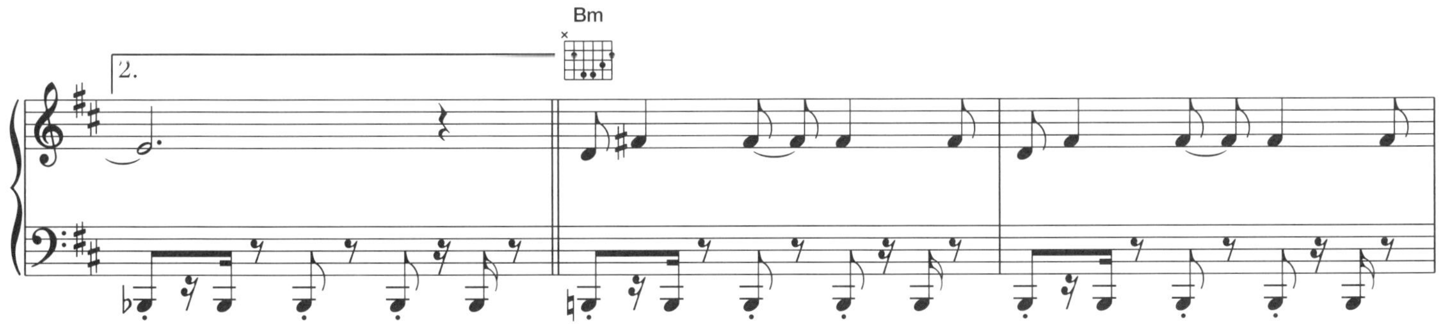
Bm
2.

Dm
Gm
3fr

Bb
D.S. al Coda
2. Sweet lit - tle girl,____

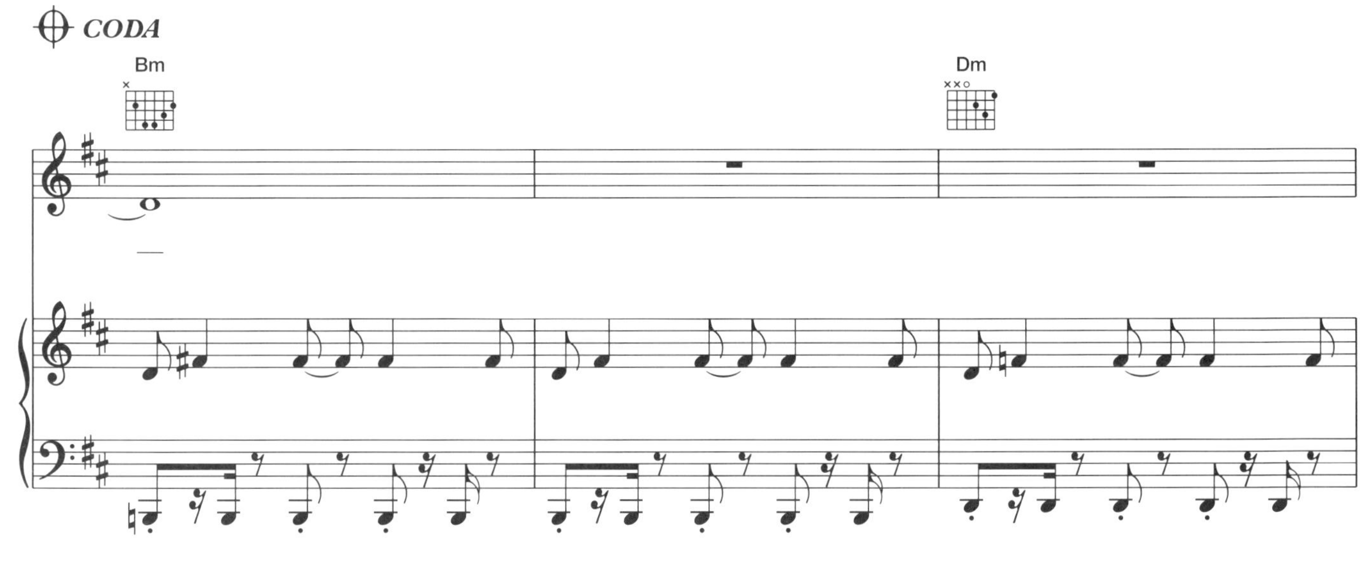
CODA
Bm
Dm

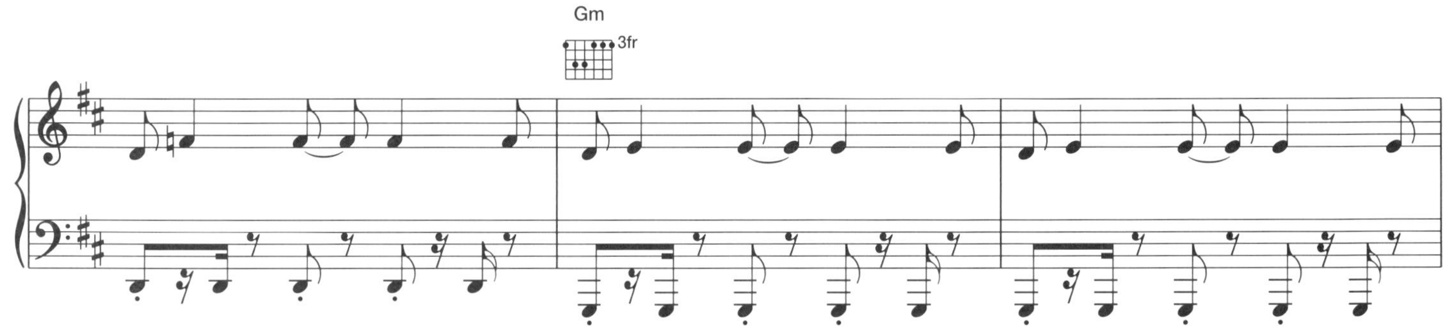
Gm
3fr

B♭
Bm
You're be - hind_ the wheel. ____________ Drive,

Dm
drive a - ny - where,__ do what you want,

Gm
Bb
you're be - hind the wheel.
Bm
Be-hind the wheel, I'm in the hands of fate,
Dm
Gm
fade out
to - night,
Bb
you're be - hind the wheel.

# Personal Jesus

Words and Music by<br>Martin Gore

41
2.
A    G#    F#m
F#m
Feel-ing un-known and you're all___ a - lone,___ flesh___
Take se-cond best,__ put me to___ the test,___ things
A    E    Bm
___ and bone__ by the te - le - phone. Lift up the re - cei - ver, I'll make
on your chest, you need to con - fess.___ I will de - li - ver, you know
F#m/C#    Dmaj7    F#m
___ you a be - lie - ver.___
___ I'm a for - giv - er.___

G#7
Gmaj7
F#m
1.
2.
Reach out, touch faith.
Your own
F#m
per - son-al    Je - sus.
per - son-al    Je - sus.
Bm
1.
A
G#
Some-one to hear your    prayers,    some-one who cares.
Some-one to hear your    prayers,    some-one who's there.
Your own
2.
A
G#7
D
N.C.
Breath vocal sound

F#m
Feel-ing un-known and you're all _____ a - lone, flesh ___ and bone by the te - le - phone.
A
E
Bm
F#m/C#
Dmaj7
F#m
Lift up the re-cei-ver, I'll make ___ you a be-lie - ver. ________

I will de-li-ver, you know __ I'm a for-giv-er. __
Your own __ per - son-al Je -
Reach out, touch faith.
- sus. __
Reach out, touch faith.
play 4 times
Reach out and touch faith.

# Enjoy The Silence



Words and Music by
Martin Gore

Cm
E♭m
in - to__ my lit-tle world.
words are tri-vi - al. __
Pain - ful to me,
Plea - sures re - main,
pierce right through me,
so does the pain,
A♭
Fm
can't you un-der-stand,
words are mean-ing-less,
oh my lit-tle girl.
and for-get-ta - ble.
All I ev-er want - ed,
A♭
Cm
E♭/B♭
all I ev-er need - ed is here
in my___ arms.
Fm
A♭
Cm
Words are ve - ry__ un - nec - es - sa - ry,__ they can on - ly do__

Fm
Ab
Cm
Eb/Bb
All I ev-er want - ed, all I ev-er need-ed is here in my arms.
Fm
Ab
Cm
1.
Cb
Words are ve - ry un - nec - es - sa - ry, they can on - ly do harm.
2.
Cb
Fm
Ab
Cm
harm.
repeat to fade
Eb/Bb
Fm
Ab
Cm
Eb/Bb
(vocal ad lib. from 2nd time)
Ah, ah . . .

# Policy Of Truth

Words and Music by
Martin Gore

Cm7    F5  Cm  Eb5    Ab
what you're be-ing put through.__ It's__ just time to pay__ the price for not_
been if you'd on-ly lied.____ It's__ too late_ to change e-vents, it's time

Fm    Bb    G7/B
__ lis-ten-ing to____ ad-vice and de-cid-ing in__ your youth__ on the po-li — cy_
__ to face_ the con-se-quence for de-liv-er-ing__ the proof__ in the po-li — cy_

Cm  Eb    Ab  Cm    Eb  Ab  Cm
__ of truth.
__ of truth.

1.  Eb  Ab  Cm    Eb  Ab  Cm
2. Things could

2.
Eb                    Fm                    Cm          Eb
Ne - ver a - gain___ is what___ you swore the time___ be - fore.___

Ab          Cm          Eb                    Fm
Ne - ver a - gain___ is what___ you swore_ the time

Cm          Eb          Ab          Cm          Eb
1st time only
___ be - fore.___

Ab          Cm          N.C.          Cm

3. Now you're stand - ing there tongue tied,
you'd bet - ter learn your les - son well.
Hide what you have to hide and tell what you have to tell.

Ab/C
Cm
Ab
You'll see____ your prob - lems mul - ti - plied___ if you___
Fm
Bb
___ con - tin - ual - ly_____ de - cide___ to faith - ful - ly____ pur - sue___
G7/B
Cm
Eb
Ab
Cm
___ the po - li - cy_____ of truth.__
Eb
Fm
Cm
Eb
Ne - ver a - gain___ is what____ you swore the time____ be - fore.____

Ab  Cm  Eb  Fm
Ne - ver a - gain___ is what___ you swore___ the time
Cm  Eb  Ab  Cm  Eb  Ab  Cm
1st time only
be - fore.
Cm  Eb  Ab  Cm  Eb  Ab  Cm
Eb  Ab  Cm  Eb  Ab  Cm

Eb    Ab    Cm              Eb    Ab    Cm
Ne-ver a - gain__ is what__ you swore the time__ be-fore.__

Eb    Ab    Cm              Eb    Ab    Cm
Ne-ver a - gain__ is what__ you swore the time__ be-fore.__

Cm    Eb    Ab    Cm        Eb    Ab    Cm
Ne-ver a - gain is what__ you swore the time__ be-fore.__

repeat to fade
Eb    Ab    Cm              Eb    Ab    Cm
Ne-ver a - gain__ is what__ you swore the time__ be-fore.__

# World In My Eyes

Words and Music by
Martin Gore

Let me show you the world in my eyes.
Let me show you the world in my eyes.
That's all there
is, no-thing more than you can feel now, that's all there is.

Let me  put you on a ship,  on a  long, long trip,  your__ lips close to my
__ lips.  All the  is-lands in the o - cean,__  all the  hea-vens in the mo - tion.
__  Let me  show you the world in my eyes.__

That's all there is, no-thing more than you can touch now, that's all there is.
Let me show you the world in my eyes,
let me show you the world in my eyes.
repeat to fade

# I Feel You

Words and Music by
Martin Gore

I feel
I feel
I feel
you, with - in my mind.
you, the joy it brings.
you, each breath you take.
Dm
G
You take me there you take me where the king-dom
Where hea - ven waits, those gol - den gates and back a -
Where an - gels sing and spread their wings, my love's on
Am
Dm
G
comes. You take me to and lead me through Ba - by - lon.
gain. You take me to and lead me through ob - li - vi - on.
high. You take me home to glo - ry's throne by and by.

Am
Dm    F    G    C
This is the morn-ing of our love.
Am
Dm    F    G    C
It's just the dawn-ing of our love.
Am
To Coda
1.
2.
(2.) I
I
Dm    C    F#m    F    Am
feel _________ you, _ your pre-cious soul and I am whole.

63
Dm
C
F#m
I feel ________ you, _ your ris - ing sun, my king-dom
F
Am
comes, my king-dom comes.
R.H. R.H. R.H. sim.

D.S. al Coda
CODA
Dm F G C
This is the morn-ing of our love.
(3.) I
Am
Dm F G C
It's just the dawn-ing of our love.
Am
Am
Repeat to Fade

# Walking In My Shoes

Gm
Dm
tell you 'bout the things they put _ me through, _ the pain I've been sub - ject - ed to, _
C
Dm
Gm
but the Lord him-self _ would blush. _ The count-less feasts laid at _ my feet, _ for -
Dm
C
bid - den fruits for me _ to eat, _ but I think your pulse would start to rush. _
Dm
C/D
Dm
Now I'm not look-ing for ab - so - lu - tion,

C/D
Dm
C/D
for - give-ness for the things I __ do, __ but be-fore you come to
F
Db-5
Bb7
a - ny con-clu - sions try walk-ing in my ____ shoes,
Gm7
Dm
try walk-ing in my ____ shoes. You'll stum-ble in my foot steps,
A/C#
Bbmaj7
Gm9
keep the same ap-point-ments I kept, if you try walk-ing in my __

Bbmaj7
C6
Dm7
shoes,
if you try walk-ing in my ___ shoes.
Gm9
Bbmaj9
Dm7
C6
(2.) Mor - if you try walk-ing in my ___
Ped
Ped
Ped
Bbmaj7
C6
Dm
shoes,
try walk-ing in my ___ shoes.

A/C#
Bbmaj7
Gm9
C
Dm
C
Dm
C
Dm
C
Dm
C
Now I'm not look-ing for ab-so-lu- tion,
for -give-ness for the things I ___ do, ___ but be-fore you come to

F
Db-5
Bb7
a - ny con - clu - sions          try walk-ing in my ___ shoes,
Gm7
Dm
try walk -ing in my ___ shoes. You'll stum-ble in my      foot - steps,
A/C#
Bbmaj7
Gm9
keep the same ap-point-ments I kept,          if you try walk-ing in my___
Bbmaj7
1. C6
2. C6
___ shoes.          You'll stum-ble in my          Try walk -ing in my___

*VERSE 2:*
Morality would frown upon,
Decency look down upon
The scapegoat fate's made of me.
But I promise now my judge and jurors,
My intentions couldn't have been purer,
My case is easy to see.

I'm not looking for a clearer conscience,
Peace of mind after what I've been through.
And before we talk of any repentance,
Try walking in my shoes,
Try walking in my shoes.

# Condemnation

Words and Music by
Martin Gore

E
G#m
B+
If for ho-nest-y you want a-po-lo-gies
If you see pu-ri-ty, as im-ma-tu-ri-ty,
I don't sym-pa-thise
well it's no sur-prise
E
G#m
B+
if for kind-ness you sub-sti-tute blind-ness,
please o-pen your eyes.
Em6
1.
B
E B
E B
2.
B
E B
F. B
Repeat to Fade
F#7
(2.) Con-dem- Ah ah ah ah.

# In Your Room

Words and Music by
Martin Gore

Em/C#
D#m/C#
D/C#
C#m
C#m
C#m
(1.) In your room,
where time stands still or moves at your

G#m/C#
will,
will you, let the morn-ing come soon,
A/C#
or will you leave me ly-ing here
C#m
in your fa-vour-ite dark - ness,
your
E#m
fa-vour-ite half - light,
A
your fa-vour-ite con - scious-ness,

F#m
your fa-vour-ite slave? __________
1. C#m
C#sus2
4th Fret
F#m/C#
C#m
C#sus2
F#m/C#
2. C#m
(2.) In your __ I'm hang-ing on your words

C#sus2
F#m
F#m7
liv - ing on your breath, feel -ing with your skin will I al -ways
Repeat on %.
C#m
C#sus2
be here? I'm hang -ing on your words, liv -ing on your breath,
F#m
F#m7
feel - ing with your skin. Will I al - ways
C#m
C#sus2
F#m
be here? Hang-ing on your words, liv-ing on your breath, feel-ing with your

VERSE 2:
In your room,
Where souls disappear,
Only you exit here.
Will you lead me to your armchair
Or leave me lying here:
Your favourite innocence,
Your favourite prize.
Your favourite smile.
Your favourite slave?

VERSE 3:
In your room,
Your burning eyes
Cause flames to arise;
Will you let the fire die down soon
Or will I always be here,
Your favourite passion,
Your favourite game,
Your favourite mirror,
Your favourite slave?

# Barrel of a Gun

Words and Music by
Martin Gore

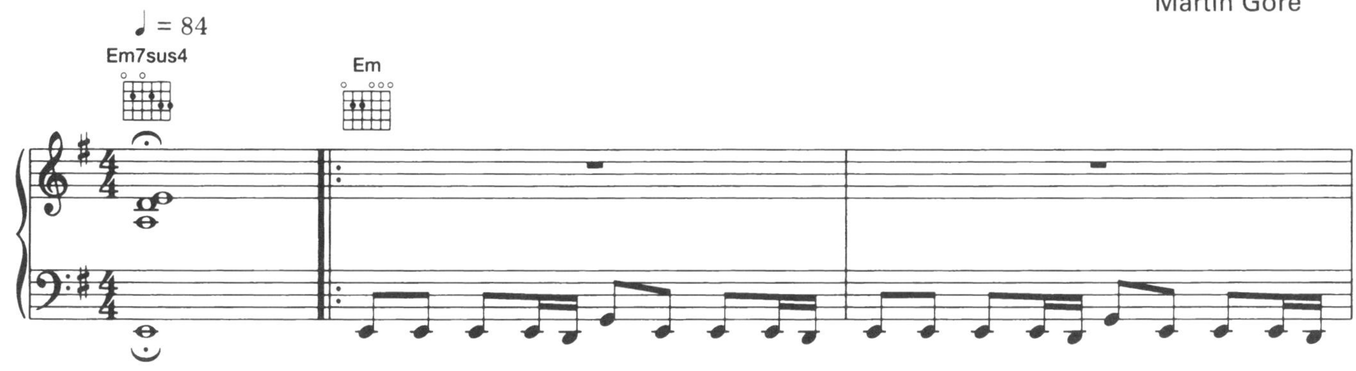

sleep that does-n't come?
-fied, won't be de - nied.
Mm.
Mm.
Mm.
Mm.
This
An
twist - ed, tor - tured mess, this bed of sin - ful - ness who's long - ing for some
un - bear - a - ble pain, a beat-ing in my brain that leaves the mark of
rest and feel-ing numb.
Cain right here in - side.

Em7
What do you ex-pect of me, what is it you want?
What am I sup-posed to do? When ev-ery-thing that I've done
What-ev-er you've planned for me,
Is lead-ing me to con-clude
1.
A G F Em
I'm not the one.
I'm not the one.
2.
G F Em
What-ev-er I've done,

I've been star-ing down the bar-rel of a gun.
What-ev - er I've done,
I've been star-ing down the bar-rel of a gun.
What-ev - er I've done.
(What-ev - er, what-ev - er)

Em
Is there some-thing you need ___ from me?
Are you hav-ing your fun? ___
I ne-ver a-greed ___ to be
A
your ho - ly one. ___
G   F   Em
What-ev - er I've done,
A   G   F
I've been star-ing down the bar-rel of a gun. ___
C   B

What-ev - er I've done, ___
(what-ev - er, what-ev - er)
I've been star-ing down the bar-rel of a gun. ___
What-ev - er I've done, ___ (what-ev - er, what-ev -
I've been star-ing down the bar-rel of a gun. ___
- er)
repeat to fade

# It's No Good

Words and Music by
Martin Gore

Abmaj7
Ab/Bb
Cm
- ten in the stars a - bove,_____ the Gods de - cree
- ing to my o - pen arms,_____ when will you re -al -ise,_____

Cm7sus4/Bb
Abmaj7
Ab/Bb
you'll be right___ here by___ my side,___ right next to me.
do we have to wait till our worlds col - lide,___ o - pen up your eyes.

Cm
Cm7/Bb
Abmaj9
You can run_____ but you can -not hide.
You can't turn back the tide_

Ab/Bb
Cm
Don't say you want___ me, don't say you need___ me, don't say you love

__ me,  it's un-der - stood. __ Don't say you're hap - py  out there with-out

__ me,  I know you can't __ be  'cause it's no  good. _____

Cm7


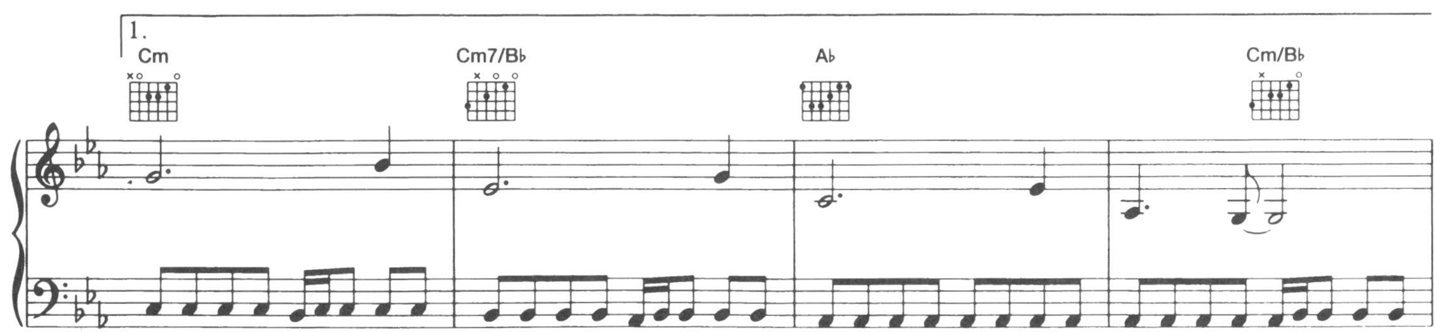

1.
Cm          Cm7/B♭          A♭          Cm/B♭

Cm
Cm7/B♭
A♭
Cm/B♭
I'll be fine
2.
Instrumental ad lib.
Cm
I'm going to take my
Cm
A♭/C
Adim/C
time,
I have all_____ the time__ in the world

Ab/C
Cm
Ab/C
to make you mine.
It is writ-
Adim/C
Ab/C
Cm
- ten in the stars a - bove.
Cm7/Bb
Ab
Cm/Bb
Cm
Cm7/Bb
Ab
Cm/Bb
Don't say you want

Cm
_ me,      don't say you need _ me,      don't say you love _ me,      it's

un-der - stood._ Don't say you're hap - py      out there with-out _ me,      I know you can't

1.
2.
_ be      'cause it's no   good._ Don't say you want   it's no   good._____

Cm7
repeat ad lib. to fade

# Home

Words and Music by
Martin Gore

Ab  Ab7
Here is a page   from the emp -
and the sick  -  li - est sweet
Fb/Ab   Ab   Ab7   Fb/Ab
- ti - est stage   a cage   or the hea - vi - est cross   ev - er made   a gauge
smell-ing sheets   that cling   to the backs   of my knees   and my feet,   well I'm drown-
Ab   Ab7   Fb/Ab   Dbm
__ of the dead - li - est trap   ev - er laid.____ And I
- ing in time__ to a des   per - ate beat.____ And I   thank you____   for
Fm   Ab   Bbm   Db   Fm   Ab
4fr   4fr
bring-ing me here,____   for   show-ing me home,____   for   sing-ing these tears,____   fin -

Db
Bb7/D
Dbm
1.
Ab
Ab7
- al - ly I've found that I belong here.
Fb/Ab
Ab
Ab7
Fb/Ab
The heat
2.
Bbm
Bbm7/Ab
Gb
Bbm/F
F7/Eb
Feels like home,
I should have known
Gb
Bbm/F
Bbm7b5
Ab
Ab7
from my first breath.

Fb  Ab  Ab9  Fb/Ab
Ab  Ab7  Fb/Ab  Ab  Ab7
God send the on - ly true friend I call mine, pre-tend that __ I'll make a-mends
Fb/Ab  Ab  Ab7  Fb/Ab
the next time, be-friend __ the __ glo - ri-ous end of the line. ______ And I
Dbm  Fm 4fr  Ab  Bbm  Db
thank you ________ for bring-ing me here, ______ for show-ing me home, ______ for

Fm
Ab
Db
Bb7/D
Dbm
sing-ing these tears,________ fi - nal - ly I've__ found that I________ be - long__


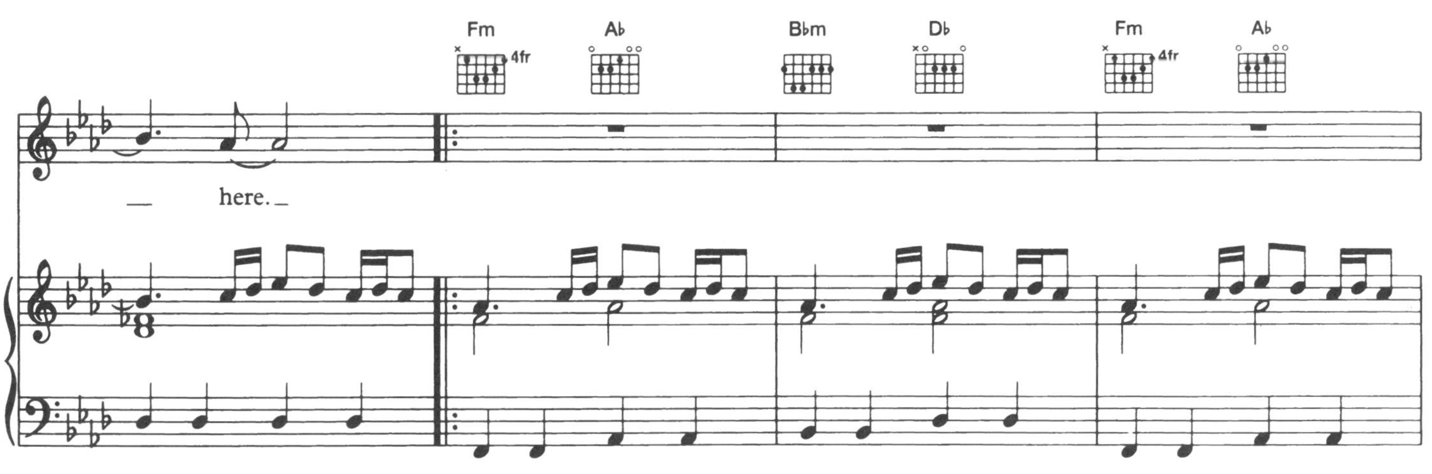

Fm
Ab
Bbm
Db
Fm
Ab
__ here. __

Db
Bb7/D
Dbm
1.
Bbm7b5

2.
Bbm
Db
Fm
Bbm
Db
Fm
repeat ad lib. to fade

# Useless

Words and Music by
Martin Gore

Well it's a - bout_______ time
Watch the clock on the_______ wall
Here I stand the ac - cused

Ebm
Gb
Cbmaj7
Ebm/Bb
it's be - gin-ning to_______ hurt,
feel the slow-ing of_______ time,
with your fist in my_______ face,

Ebm
Gb
Cbmaj7
time you made up your_______ mind
hear a voice in the_______ hall
feel - ing ti - red and_______ bruised


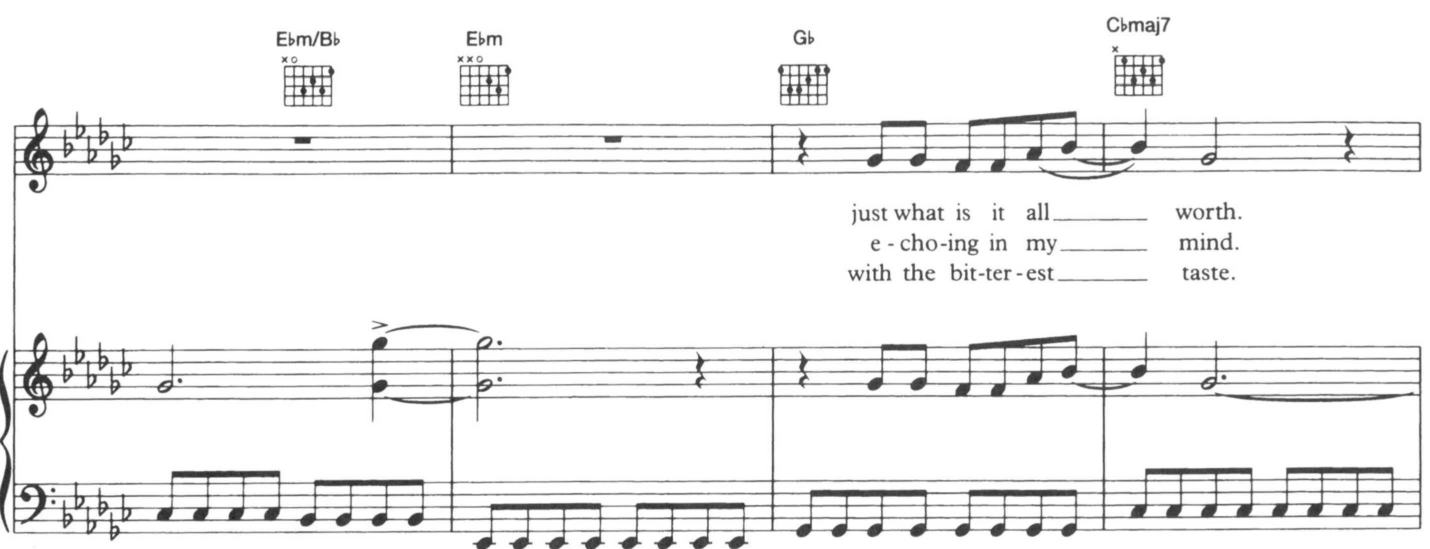

Ebm/Bb
Ebm
Gb
Cbmaj7
just what is it all_______ worth.
e - cho-ing in my_______ mind.
with the bit-ter-est_______ taste.

E♭m/B♭
B♭
C♭
℅ All my use-less ad - vice,
All your stu-pid i - deals,
B♭
C♭
B♭
all my hang-ing a - round,
got your head in the clouds,
all your cut-ting down to size,
you should see how it feels
C♭
D♭
to Coda ⊕
all my bring-ing you down.
with your feet on the ground.
1.
C♭
B♭
2.
C♭

Bb
Cb
Bb
Cb
Bb
Cb
Db
Cb
Bb
Ebm
D.S. al Coda
CODA
Cb
Bb
All your stu-pid i - deals,

Cb
Bb
Cb
got your head in the clouds,
Bb
Cb
Db
you should see how it feels
Cb
Bb
with your feet on the ground.
Ebm

# Only When I Lose Myself

Words and Music by
Martin Gore

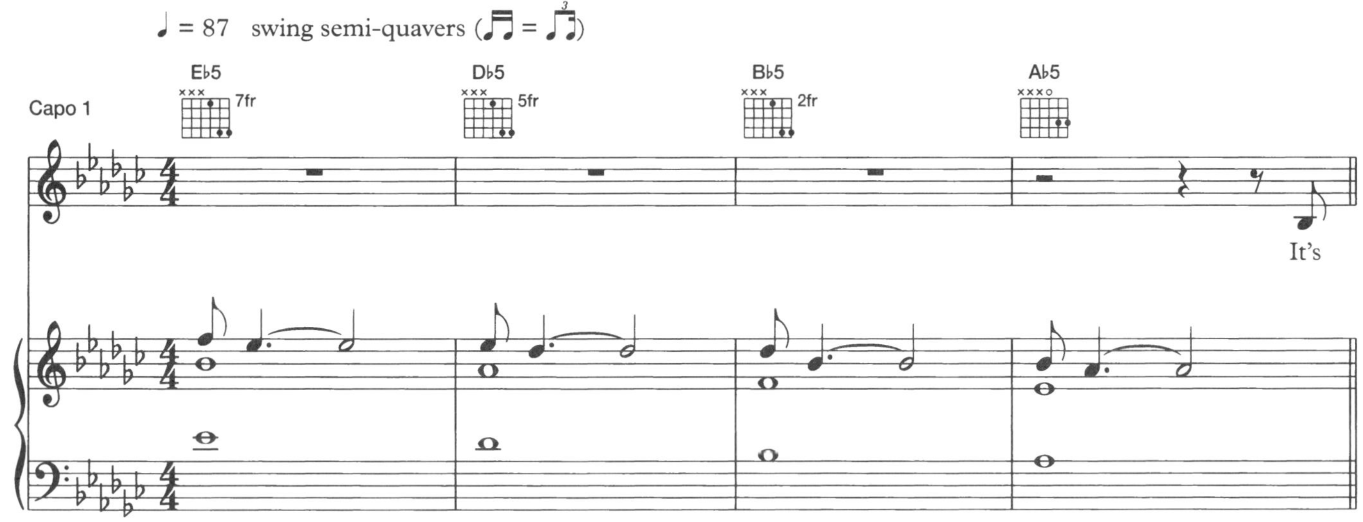

Bb5/Eb
Ab5/Eb
Eb5
Db5
find my - self,__ I find my - self.__
Bb5
Ab5
Eb5
Db5
Bb5
Ab5
Abm/Eb
Fbmaj7
Abm/Eb
Some-thing beau-ti-ful is hap-pen-ing in-side for__ me,____ some-thing sen-su-al, it's
Fbmaj7
Dbm/Eb
Abm
full of fire and my-ste-ry.____ I feel hyp-no-tised,__ I feel pa-ra-lysed,

103
Dbm    Cb    Cb/Bb    Abm/Eb
I have found hea - ven. There's a thou-sand rea-sons why I

Fbmaj7    Abm/Eb    Fbmaj7
should-n't spend my time with you. For ev-ery rea-son not to be here I can think of two.

Dbm/Eb    Abm    Dbm
Keep me hang-ing on, feel-ing no-thing's wrong, in-side your hea -

Cb    Cb/Bb    N.C.
- ven. It's

N.C.
straight

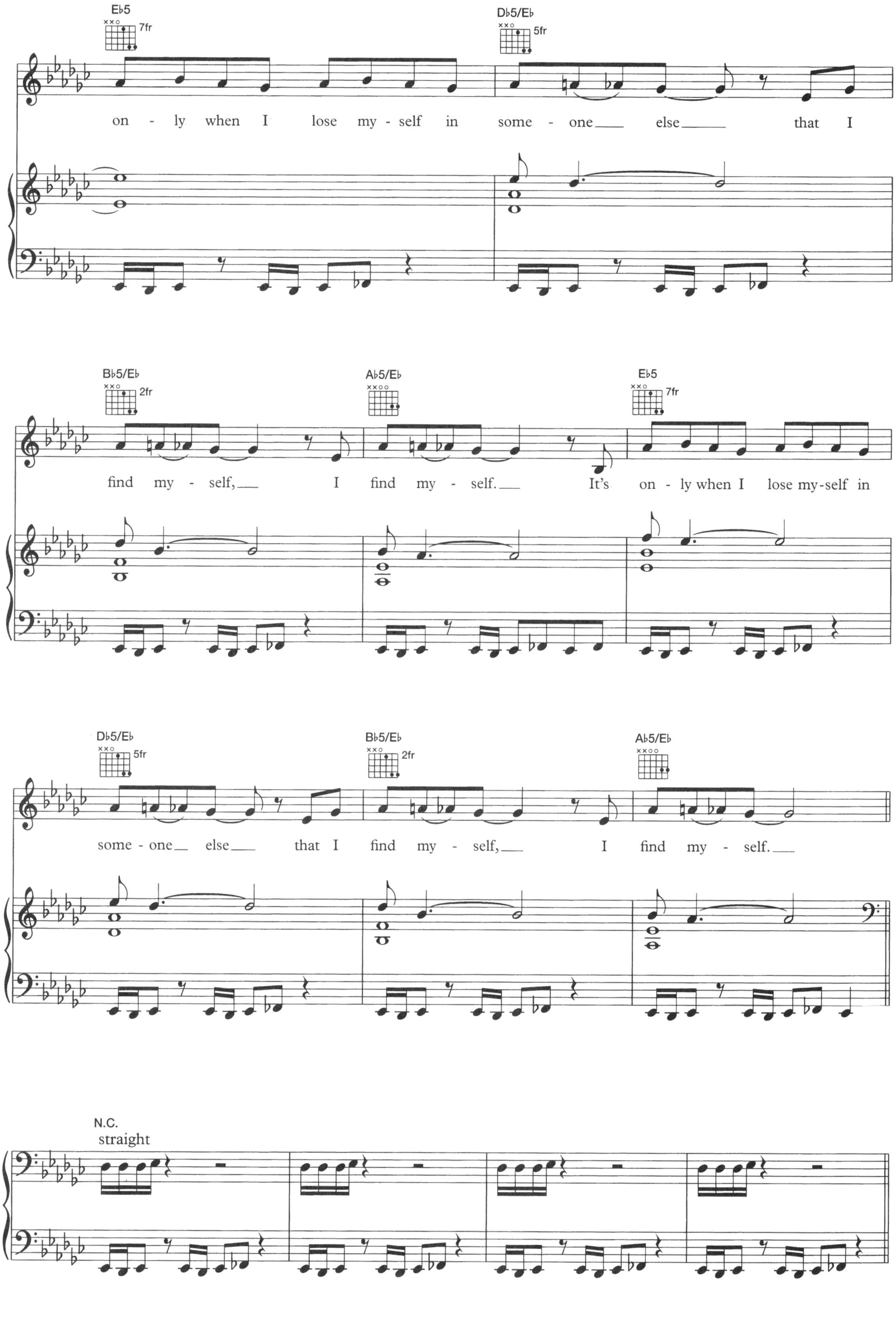

on - ly when I lose my-self in some - one___ else___ that I find my - self,___ I find my - self.___ It's on - ly when I lose my-self in some - one___ else___ that I find my - self,___ I find my - self.___

I can feel the emp-ti-ness in - side me, fade and dis-ap - pear. There's a feel-ing of con-
-tent-ment now that you are here. I feel sa-tis - fied, I be-long in - side
your vel - vet hea - ven.
Did I need to sell my soul for plea-sure like this.

Did I have to lose con-trol____ to trea-sure your kiss.____
Did I need to place my heart_ in the palm of your hand.
Be-fore I could e - ven start
to un - der-stand.____ It's

Eb5
Db5/Eb
Bb5/Eb
on - ly when I lose my-self in some - one___ else___ that I find my - self,___ I
Ab5/Eb
Eb5
Db5/Eb
find my - self.___ It's on - ly when I lose my-self in some - one___ else___ that I
Bb5/Eb
1.
Ab5/Eb
2.
Ab5/Eb
find my - self,___ I find my - self.___ It's find my - self.___
Eb5
Db5
Bb5
Ab5

# Little 15

♩ = 109
Em
B/D#
Em
1. Lit - tle fif - teen,
(2.)
B/D#
you help her for - get the world out - side,
why take the smooth with the rough?
the world out - side,
When things run smooth
Em
B/D#
you're not part of it yet.
it's al - rea - dy more than e - nough.

Em
And if you could drive,___ you could drive her a-way___
She knows your mind___ is not yet in league
B/D#
4fr
to a hap-pi-er place,___
with the rest of the world___
Em
B/D#
4fr
to a hap-pi-er day___ that ex-ists in your mind_
and it's lit-tle in-trigues.___ Do you un-der-stand,
Am
and in your smile.___
do you know what she means?
B

Am
She could es - cape ____ there     just for a while,
As     time goes by, ____     and when you've seen what she's seen, ____
B
N.C.
1.
Em
____     lit - tle fif - teen. ____
____     you will,     lit - tle fif - teen.
B7/D#
Em
B7/D#
2. Lit - tle fif - teen

2.
C#m
G#7/B#
C#m
G#7/B#
F#m
G#7
F#m
G#7
Ebm
Lit - tle fif - teen,______________ why does she have to de - fend

B♭/D
E♭m
her feel-ings in - side,___
B♭/D
why pre - tend?___
She's not had a life,_
E♭m
B♭/D
___ a life of near miss-es.
E♭m
Now all that she wants___
is three lit - tle

Bb/D
Abm
wish-es.
She wants to see with your eyes,
Bb
she wants to smile with your smile.
She wants a nice sur-prise
Abm
Bb
ev-ery once in a while.
1.
She wants to see with your eyes,
2. N.C.
Lit-tle fif-teen.
Eb

# Everything Counts

E7
con - tract there's no ___ turn - ing back. The turn - ing point of a ca-
sto - ry of it ___ all. Pic - ture it now,
Dm7
Am
-reer ___ in Ko - rea ___ be - ing in - sin - cere.
see just how the lies ___ and de - ceit gained a little more pow - er.
E7
Am
The ho - li - day was fun - packed, the
Con - fi - dence, ta - ken in by a
E7
A7
C
G
con - tract still in - tact. The grab - bing hands
sun - tan and a grin. ___

grab all they can, __ all for them-selves, af - ter all. __ The
grab - bing hands grab all they can, __ all for them-selves,
af - ter all. __ It's a com-pe-ti-tive ____ world.
Ev-ery-thing counts in large ____ a - mounts.

G
F
Am
G
F
Am
G
F
Am
2.
G
F
Am
G
F
2. The
Dm
F
G
A♭
4fr
Am
C
Ev - ery - thing counts in large_____ a - mounts.
G
F
Dm
F
G
A♭
4fr
Ev - ery - thing counts in large_____ a - mounts.

The
grab - bing hands      grab all they can,___      ev - ery-thing counts in large___ a - mounts. The

2.
G    A♭    C    G    F    Am
2nd time only
a - mounts.
Ev - ery-thing,    ev - ery-thing.
Dm    Fmaj7
1.
G    A♭
2.
G    A♭
Ev - ery-thing,    ev - ery-thing. The
C    G    F    Am    Dm    Fmaj7
grab - bing hands    grab all they can,    ev - ery-thing counts    in    large
1.
G    A♭
2.
G    A♭    C    G
a - mounts. The    a - mounts.

F    Am    Dm    Fmaj7    G    A♭
C    G    F    Am    Dm    Fmaj7
G    A♭    C    G    F    Am
The grab - bing hands__ grab all they can,__
Dm    Fmaj7    G    A♭    C    G    F    Am
ev - ery-thing counts in large___ a - mounts. The grab - bing hands grab all they can,__
Dm    Fmaj7    1. G    A♭    2. G    A♭
ev - ery-thing counts in large___ a - mounts. The ___ a - mounts.